A WORLD OF HOLIDAYS

EASTER

A WORLD OF HOLIDAYS

Easter

Catherine Chambers

RSVP
RAINTREE
STECK-VAUGHN
PUBLISHERS
The Steck-Vaughn Company

Austin, Texas

Published by Raintree Steck-Vaughn Publishers,
an imprint of Steck-Vaughn Company

Library of Congress Cataloging-in-Publication Data

Chambers, Catherine.
    Easter / Catherine Chambers.
        p.   cm. — (A world of holidays)
    Includes bibliographical references (p. 30) and index.
    Summary: Introduces the holiday of Easter and explains how it is celebrated all over the world.

    ISBN 0-8172-4615-0 (hardcover)
    ISBN 0-8172-3886-7 (softcover)
    1. Easter —Juvenile literature.   [1. Easter.   2. Jesus Christ—Resurrection.   3. Holidays.]   I. Title.
II. Series.
GT4935.C48   1998
394.2667—dc21   97-18328
                                                           CIP
                                                            AC

Printed in Spain
Bound in United States
1 2 3 4 5 6 7 8 9 0   01 00 99 98 97

ACKNOWLEDGMENTS

Editors: Su Swallow, Pam Wells
Design: T.J. Graphics
Production: Jenny Mulvanny

The publishers would like to thank the Reverend Martin J. Burne, O.S.B., Saint Mary's Abbey, Morristown, New Jersey, for reading and advising on the manuscript.

For permission to reproduce copyright material, the author and publishers gratefully acknowledge the following:

cover: © Superstock
title page: Richard Passmore/Tony Stone
page 6 (top) Rohan/Tony Stone (bottom) Tony Gervis/Robert Harding Picture Library page 7 (top) Circa Photo Library (bottom) John Hatt/Hutchison Library page 8 Trip/H Gariety page 9 (top) Trip/ O Semenenko (bottom) Richard Passmore/Tony Stone page 10 Anthony King page 11 (top) Robert Harding Picture Library (bottom) Eric Lawrie/Hutchison Library page 12 (left) Trip/ C Caffrey (right) Trip/J Garrett page 13 Circa Photo Library page 14 Travel Ink/Nick Battersby page 15 (left) Trip/T Bognar (right) Eric Lawrie/Hutchison Library page 16 Circa Photo Library page 17 (left) Trip/M Lee (right) H Rogers/Trip page 18 (left) Anthony King (top right) Andzey Zvoznikov/Hutchison Library page 19 (top) Tony Stone Images, USA (bottom) Robert Harding Picture Library page 20 Rosemary Evans/Tony Stone page 21 (top) Trip/A Gasson (bottom) Trip/Viesti Collection page 22 (top) Trip/J Stanley (bottom) Trip/J Stanley page 23 Trip/ G Gunnarsson page 24 Hutchison Library page 25 (top right) Trip/G Gunnarsson (bottom) Thierry Dosogne/Image Bank page 26 (top) Trip/Viesti Collection (bottom) Circa Photo Library page 27 Brad Markel/Gamma Liaison Network (bottom) Jerome Tisne/Tony Stone Images page 28 and 29 Alan Towse

Contents

Born Again

Easter is the most important and joyful holiday, or festival, for Christians. It falls in the season of spring — a time to celebrate new life.

The City of Jerusalem is where Jesus died and rose from the dead.

THE BEGINNING OF CHRISTIANITY

About 2,000 years ago in Palestine, there lived a religious teacher called Jesus Christ. Christians believe that he was the Son of God. Easter celebrates the time when Jesus rose from the dead in Jerusalem, a city in Palestine. It joyfully celebrates renewed life. Christians believe that one day, they will rise from death, too. This makes the Easter holiday a festival of hope.

After Jesus rose from the dead, he gathered his followers around him. He prepared them to spread his teachings throughout the world. This is when the Christian religion really began.

WHEN DO WE CELEBRATE?

An important celebration was taking place in Jerusalem when Jesus rose from the dead. This was the Festival of Passover. It is celebrated by followers of the Jewish faith. So the first Christians added Easter to this ancient festival. Passover takes place in March or April. The time depends on the phases of the moon.

A church in Greece is decorated for Easter.

Some Christian churches celebrate Easter at a different time from others. Eastern Orthodox Christians come from parts of central and eastern Europe. They celebrate Easter later than other churches.

Christians hold services and customs throughout Holy Week. This week ends on Easter Sunday, when Jesus rose from the dead. There are sad celebrations in Holy Week. But there are joyful ones, too!

Before the Easter festival began, other festivals were held at this time of year. From Iran, across North Africa, and into Europe, people celebrated the newness of spring.

Some of the customs have survived until today. They fit in well with the Christian celebration of new life at Easter.

An Easter egg is the perfect gift for this priest.

In Guatemala, a brilliant Easter procession slowly moves along.

7

The Easter Story

This is a story that begins with Jesus Christ's suffering and death. But it ends with his triumph and rebirth at Easter.

FROM CARPENTER TO TEACHER

Jesus Christ was a carpenter from Palestine. He belonged to the Jewish faith. But Christians believe that Jesus was also the Son of God.

Jesus had come to Earth to teach people how to live better lives. But Jesus knew that his beliefs would make some people angry. He knew that, in the end, these people would want him dead.

But Jesus continued spreading his message of love for God and for all people on Earth. He also performed amazing miracles. Jesus gathered around him 12 faithful followers, known as the apostles. They became the earliest disciples — the first Christian teachers.

Christ appears to his disciples in this stained-glass window of a church.

THE LAST DAYS

The last week of Christ's life was full of joy — then full of pain. Now famous, he rode one Sunday into Jerusalem. He was carried on a donkey — a symbol of peace. The crowds lined the streets, cheering and waving palms.

But by the following Thursday, his life was near its end. Some of the Jewish leaders were angry with him. They persuaded the Roman rulers to arrest him. Worse, one of Christ's own apostles, Judas, showed the Roman soldiers where to find him.

Christ was tried, beaten, and finally, on Friday, he was hung on a cross. His sad friends laid him in a tomb. They thought this was the end. But the next Sunday, one of his faithful women followers saw him near his empty tomb. Jesus then prepared his disciples to go out into the world and teach others. Finally, he joined God in heaven. Today, Holy Week reminds Christians of this story of long ago.

A Russian bronze icon with colored enamels shows Christ dying on the cross.

Christ carries his own cross on this stone carving in Jerusalem.

VITTORIA GISMONDI PELLICENA D.T.S. A RICORDO DEI SUOI GENITORI

Processions of Palms

On the Sunday before Easter, crowds of people lined the streets of Jerusalem, waving palms and cheering. Jesus and his apostles were entering the city! That day is remembered as Palm Sunday.

WAVING PALMS

In those days, people waved palms when someone really important arrived. Jesus had become very famous. So the crowds waved palms as he rode into Jerusalem on a donkey.

At this time in many churches, dried palms, or pieces of palm, are blessed. This means they they are made holy. Priests and other members of the church hold the palms up high.

The palms are paraded through the church. Sometimes they are waved in processions through the streets. You can see this especially in South and Central America, and southern Europe.

WEARING PALMS

In many parts of the world, small pieces of dried palm are twisted and tied into the

On the morning of Palm Sunday, priests carry palms through the streets of a Spanish town.

10

◀ On Palm Sunday in Colombia, people are carrying a heavy statue of Christ in a long procession.

▼ There are palm fronds for everyone in Ecuador.

shape of a cross. They are then given out to all the people in church on Palm Sunday. Some people hold them, while others pin them onto their clothes. In some churches, the palms are kept until the following February — the solemn Christian season of Lent. This is the time Jesus spent in the desert, where he fought against evil. On the first day of Lent, Ash Wednesday, the old palms are burned. Palm ashes are drawn on people's foreheads in the shape of a cross.

In parts of Europe, such as France and Belgium, a small piece of boxwood used to be given out instead of palm. Some people placed them above the doors of their houses to protect the home and the family from harm. Even the animals' stables had a piece of boxwood to keep them safe. Sometimes, palm willow or the herb, rosemary, has been used.

11

Maundy Thursday

On the Thursday before he died, Jesus and his apostles were celebrating the Jewish Festival of Passover. At the feast, Jesus taught his followers ways of remembering him.

A WAY OF REMEMBERING

"Maundy" comes from a word in the old Latin language. It means "command." The Thursday before Easter is known as Maundy Thursday, or Holy Thursday. On this day, Jesus Christ ate and drank with his followers. The meal became known as the Last Supper,

A priest gives Communion.

because Jesus died soon after. At the meal, he commanded his followers to do two simple things to remember him by.

One of the ways of remembering him was to break bread and eat it. The bread represented Christ's body. The other way was to sip some wine, which stood for Christ's blood. Christians all over the world still remember Christ in these ways. They sip wine and take bread in services known as Mass, or Communion.

SERVING THE POOR

On this day, priests often wash the feet of churchgoers. This is because Christ washed the feet of

On Maundy Thursday a Spanish lady from Seville wears her black mantilla as a sign of mourning.

his apostles on that first Maundy Thursday. The tradition began in Europe over 1,500 years ago. Then, popes, priests, kings, and queens washed the feet of twelve or more poor men or beggars.

In the United States, this special Maundy Thursday practice continues. The priest washes the feet of some of the worshipers during the Maundy Thursday service.

PANEM SCIFICAT XPC QY O SECVLA PASCAT.
ABLVIT EXTERIVS SORDES QY COB LAVAT INTVS.

The top painting from Romania shows the Last Supper. The bottom picture shows Christ washing the feet of his apostles.

Good Friday

It's a day of sadness for Christians, as they remember how Jesus died on the cross. It's also a time for being sorry for things they have done wrong.

THE DARKEST DAY

After the Last Supper on Maundy Thursday, Jesus went to the Garden of Gethsemane in Jerusalem. Here, he prayed. But it was also here that one of Jesus' own apostles, Judas, turned against him. Judas showed Roman soldiers where to find Jesus. Jesus was arrested, tried, beaten, and put to death on a cross.

This is the Garden of Gethsemane, where Jesus was arrested.

On this day, churches are stripped of all decoration. The altar is often left bare or covered with a black cloth. A simple cross, like the cross on which Christ died, is placed at the center. The church lights are turned out and no candles flicker.

Bread and wine, the symbols of Christ, are sometimes left overnight on a special altar. The altar is guarded until the next day by a few members of the church. This is to remember Christ's last night in the garden. Christ had asked his followers to keep him company throughout that night. But they just couldn't keep awake. The next day, Christ asked them, "Could you not watch with me just one hour?"

Some Christians fast on this day. Also in many churches, people sit very quietly between midday and three o'clock in the afternoon. It is believed that this is the time that Christ hung on the cross before he died.

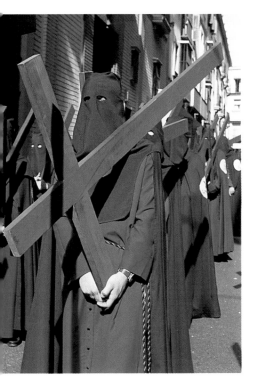

Penitents carry wooden crosses through the streets of Seville, in Spain.

A heavy statue of Jesus is carried through a town in Ecuador.

PROCESSIONS OF PENITENTS

Penitents are people who are sorry for their sins. On Good Friday in Spain, penitents cover their faces with hoods and parade slowly along the streets. In South and Central America, they walk a long way, carrying heavy wooden crosses or statues of the saints. As the sun sets in parts of Greece, funeral processions end this sad day.

15

Easter Eve

Churches are dark and silent on Holy Saturday, the day after Good Friday. But toward late evening, they slowly light up, to be ready for a joyful Easter Sunday.

CHRIST, THE LIGHT OF THE WORLD

It is Holy Saturday. Churches stay gloomy and empty until night-time. In the churches of Eastern Europe, everything starts to light up at the stroke of midnight. A flame is passed from one person to the other, so that candles and lamps can be lighted. The whole church glows.

In Roman Catholic and some other Christian Churches, a huge, bright candle is carried through the church. It shows how Jesus Christ, the Light of the World, rose from the dead and drove away the darkness of evil.

The candle is taken to the water that is used to baptize Christians. Baptism is a ceremony that makes people members of the Christian Church. The candle blesses the waters for the year ahead. Hundreds of years ago, many people became baptized at Easter with this water.

An Easter candle standing in a gleaming holder shines beside a baptismal font.

FROM SADNESS TO HAPPINESS

People celebrate Easter Eve in many different ways. In Romanian churches, a picture of Jesus is laid flat on a table. This represents Christ lying in the tomb. The members of the church then crawl under the table. They hope to leave behind their sins as they rise at the other side of the table.

At midnight in Greece, fireworks explode in the streets as people shout, "Christ is risen!"

An icon from the Lebanon shows Christ on the cross, watched by two women followers.

Fireworks mark the end of Easter Eve.

Christ Is Risen!

The church is bright with flowers and light. It is time to be happy. For Jesus Christ is risen today!

Priests wear red and gold robes at these joyful Easter celebrations in Russia.

OH, HAPPY DAY!

It is early on Easter Sunday morning as people open the church doors. What a difference they see now! There are masses of spring flowers all over the church. The altar is covered in colored cloth, and a cross rises from the center. The priest wears his or her brightest robes.

Cheerful hymns are sung in the service. The priest gets ready to remember Jesus with bread and wine, just like Jesus' first followers. The bread is placed on the most precious plate and is blessed. A gold or silver chalice holds the wine. This is a really special day.

This rare golden chalice is 900 years old.

The Hollywood Bowl, an outdoor theater in California, is the stage for an Easter service at sunrise.

On Easter Sunday, some services are held outside. In San Francisco, thousands of people flock to Mount David, the highest hill in the city. Here, they hold services under the huge 10-foot- (3-m-) high cross that towers from the top.

Inside eastern European and some modern African churches, the churchgoers search for the body of Jesus Christ in a model of the tomb. When they find the tomb empty, they shout, "Christ is risen!"

SPREADING THE FAITH

The Easter season really lasts for another 50 days. This is when Christ showed his first followers how to spread his teachings. Ascension Day falls during this time. It is the day when Christians believe Christ finally joined God in heaven.

Flower decorations are prepared at the church for Easter celebrations.

Spring Is Here at Last!

Easter time is also springtime. The trees are bursting with leaves, and the sun is starting to sizzle. It's time to celebrate — with dancing, singing, and . . . eggs!

Apple blossom and meadow flowers show that spring has arrived in Italy.

WAKE UP, WORLD!

The ancient Greeks and Romans believed that the world woke up again in spring after its long winter sleep.

At this time of the year, people in northern Europe held a spring festival of singing and dancing. This was so that the gods would bring new life to the fields and trees. The name of the festival was Ostara. It is from this that we get the name Easter.

SPRING CELEBRATIONS

Giving eggs is an ancient North African and European celebration of the new life of spring. Eggs stand for new life and spring.

One of the first signs of spring is the shrill sound of birdsongs. At the traditional E'maischen Fair in Luxembourg, china bird-flutes are sold to welcome the spring.

In the Czech Republic, girls chase boys and throw buckets of water over them — to get them bright and clean after the long winter! But they give them Easter eggs, too.

In Sweden, small girls dress up as witches and hand out Easter wishes for a few coins. Homes are decorated with twigs tipped with brightly-colored chicken feathers in praise of the new spring.

One very old way of getting ready for the sunny times ahead was to sweep out the dust of winter. Today, we call this hard work, "spring cleaning!"

Let's get clean! People throw water at each other as part of the Easter fun in Poland's capital city of Warsaw.

Dancers from Ukraine celebrate spring in traditional style.

21

Holiday Fun Today

In many parts of the world, Easter weekend is now holiday time — a time for fun! Games, music, and dancing were once part of ancient spring festivals, too.

MUSIC AND MOVEMENT

Music, dancing, and parading are old ways of celebrating spring. But Easter parades are still popular, especially in America. The most exciting is probably along New York's Fifth Avenue. It's not an organized event. Thousands of families just take to the streets and stroll along in their best clothes. Amazing Easter bonnets decorate their heads!

Bright Easter bonnets decorate a store window in New York. Which do you like best?

In the pretty Austrian city of Salzburg, a modern Easter festival is held. It is a musical celebration. Since 1967, Easter weekend in Salzburg has been filled with concerts and operas. A lot of the music played was composed by the famous composer, Mozart, who was born in Salzburg.

On the Caribbean island of Barbados, the festivities mean lots of outdoor concerts and plays by Shakespeare.

EASTER RACES

In many parts of the world, Easter is the time for races of all kinds. Try the old custom of Easter-egg racing with your friends! You each hold a spoon and balance an egg on the end. Then you race to see who can reach the finish line — without dropping the egg!

On many islands of the Caribbean, fishers, boatbuilders, and sailors are proud of their crafts and skills. Easter week is the time to race boats from bay to bay around the islands. And on the island of Tobago, there are goat and crab races too!

In Ireland and Great Britain, lovers of horseracing enjoy the most important competitions of the year. But if you want something really different, you'd better go to Lapland's famous Easter festival. There, you can watch reindeer-racing.

A friendly tug-of-war between families is a traditional way of enjoying Easter in Cyprus.

Easter Feasts

You can't have Easter without sweet desserts and candies, from rich cakes to Easter eggs!

SWEET AND STICKY

Easter cake in Greece tastes of oranges and almonds. A spicy orange sauce is poured over it. Russians eat pashka — a rich mixture of cream, soft cheese, dried fruit, and orange peel.

In the United States, it wouldn't be Easter without hot cross buns! They're soft and sticky, with currants in them. But the most important part is the cross on the top. Since the Middle Ages, it has been a symbol of Christ's cross. That's why the buns are eaten on Good Friday. But in ancient times, before Christianity, the bun meant the moon. The cross divided the moon into its four quarters. Today, the buns are eaten for several weeks before Easter.

EASTER BUNNIES — HOW DELICIOUS!

There are lots of newborn rabbits in spring. So, in parts of Europe, before Christianity, they were a spring symbol of good luck and new life. Later, people called them "Easter rabbits." Today, you can buy chocolate rabbits to eat.

Easter bread in Greece is decorated with painted hardboiled eggs!

24

A Greek family in Cyprus enjoys a traditional lamb barbecue.

Lamb is a traditional Easter food. On the morning of Easter Sunday in Greece, a soup made of lamb's stomach, rice, and lemon is eaten. The rest of the lamb is roasted for Sunday lunch.

Chocolate eggs for everyone!

I NEARLY FORGOT— EASTER EGGS!

Easter eggs are decorated, and you can play with them, too. But lots of people like to eat them. Some people peel off the patterned Easter eggshells and eat the hard-boiled egg inside. But I bet you like candy eggs best. The first chocolate eggs were made about 100 years ago in Europe.

Bright and Beautiful

Pretty patterned eggs and spring flowers brighten the Easter festival in many parts of the world.

BURSTING WITH BLOOMS

Flowers have been a part of the spring and Easter festivals for hundreds of years. On the Greek island of Corfu, the flowers of spring are made into the shape of crosses. On Good Friday, after dark, they are carried in a long procession. The bands walk with them, playing slow, sad music.

Today in New York, there are spectacular flower displays in all the large stores. Macy's, New York's most famous store, has the best flower show of all. Easter lilies bloom in the gardens at New York's Rockefeller Center, too.

Flower festivals celebrate Easter in many parts of the world. At the festival in Avrig, Romania, women parade among the floats of flowers. They wear rich velvet costumes and lots of jewelry.

▲ Easter flowers in New York.

EGG-MANIA!

Wooden eggs, ivory eggs, china eggs, and glass eggs. They've all been decorated at Easter. Hens' eggs have the raw egg blown out through a tiny hole in the shell. Then the shells are painted with bright patterns.

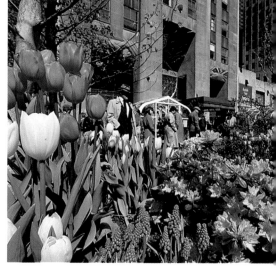

Painted Easter eggs will be hung up as decorations.

26

In Hungary, painted eggs are hung from the twigs of trees, like decorations on a Christmas tree.

In the United States, you can buy egg-painting kits. When your egg is finished, you can take it to the White House lawn in Washington, D.C. There, you can take part in egg-rolling competitions on the Great Lawn. Ancient egg-cracking competitions still take place — from Ireland in the west of Europe to Macedonia in the east. Of course, there are always those frustrating egg hunts!

An egg-rolling race is a serious matter outside the White House in Washington, D.C.

He's found it! Easter eggs are hidden in the flowers in this hunt.

Let's Celebrate!

Come and celebrate Easter! Try some egg painting. Or make a springlike Easter card.

MAKING PAINTED EGGS

Materials:
- some fresh eggs
- bright, thick paints and a paintbrush
- decorations, such as sequins and stickers
- craft glue

Directions:
1. Ask an adult to hardboil the eggs and let them cool. Or you could ask an adult to blow out the raw egg. You just need to make small holes at each end of the egg. Blow all the egg out. Then let the shell dry.
2. Paint the eggs with bright patterns and colors. You will probably need to do more than one layer of paint to get rich colors.
3. Now you can stick some decorations on the eggs, too.

MAKING AN EASTER CARD

Materials:

- colored, shiny poster paper — or you can paint white poster paper
- aluminum foil
- colored, self-stick paper — or you can color white paper
- felt-tipped pens or paints
- craft glue
- safe scissors

Directions:

1. Fold a piece of colored poster board and cut it out into a round or egg shape.
2. Cut out a cross from some shiny or plain poster paper. If the card is plain, cover it in foil. Then glue the cross onto the poster paper.
3. Cut out flowers from the self-stick paper. You could also use ordinary paper and color it in yourself.
4. Glue the flowers on the cross.

29

Glossary

altar A special table placed in a church or other place of worship.

apostles The first twelve followers of Christ who spread his teachings.

celebrate To show that a certain day or event is special.

ceremonies More solemn ways of celebrating a special day.

fast To eat only certain foods, or nothing at all — often as part of a religious custom.

mourning Feeling sorry for someone's death.

penitents People who are sorry for their sins.

popes The leaders of the Roman Catholic Church.

processions Lines of people slowly moving along.

tradition A custom, a way of doing something passed down from parents or one's culture.

tried Judged in a court of law.

Further Reading

Cura, M.J., et al. *A Path Through Easter-Pentecost for Children.* Oregon Catholic Press, 1994.

Englehart, Steve. *Easter Parade: Welcome Sweet Springtime!* Avon, 1995.

Hall. *The Easter Story.* Chariot Family, 1992.

Hibbard, Ann. *Family Celebrations at Easter.* Revell, 1994.

Kalman, Bobbie. *We Celebrate Easter.* Crabtree, 1985.

Logan, John. *Christianity.* "World Religions" series. Raintree Steck-Vaughn, 1996.

Mikolaycak, Charles. *He Is Risen: The Easter Story.* Holiday, 1985.

Sandak, Cass. *Easter.* "Holidays" series. Silver Burdett Press, 1990.

Index